Walks of Baltim[...]
Roaring Water Bay

By Damien Enright

Beautiful Castle Haven

A Merlin Press Publication

Published by Merlin Press 2000

© 2000 Damien Enright

ISBN 1 902631 04 8

Illustrations by Tish Byrne
Maps by Dan O'Connell
Cover photo by Pierce Hickey
Other photos Pierce Hickey & Damien Enright
Design by Sean O'Leary

Printed by City Print, Cork

MERLIN PRESS
The Old Courthouse, Timoleague, Co. Cork
Tel/Fax: +353 (0)23 46045. Email: merlin@eircom.net

Contents

Five easy walks - four loops and one come-and-go - in far-West Cork's lovely scenery and invigorating fresh air. Average distance from Cork 50 miles, Bantry 25, Schull 18.

Dedicated to:
my wife, Marie, and my children, friends and dog.
They have made life's roads a pleasure
and lightened my steps on the way.

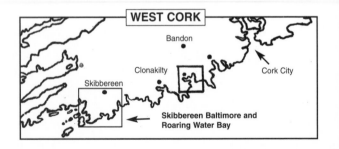

A note on walking

The Irish are big on walking. If there is one thing we have plenty of, it is back roads and fresh air.

There are the power walkers, the Walking Women of Ireland, plugging along country roads with hips and shoulders swinging, out for the exercise after an already much-exercised day. The glow of their cheeks and the litheness of their stride attests the beneficial effects of 'exercise walking'.

Irish men, on the other hand, seem oblivious to walking's cosmetic effect, an unfortunate oversight on their part. Males are not seen striding along country lanes. When we do see a male abroad, he is generally being pulled along at a heart-stopping pace by two fist-fulls of dog leads, his greyhounds taking him for a run, rather than the other way around. Other encounters will involve men in caps, with fags in mouth and pockets full of fivers, out following the road bowling, after which they will walk miles.

There are the hill walkers and long-distance route marchers, doughty folk in serious boots, with ashplants, maps and small rucksacks. To them, we owe the opening up of green roads and byways, and the mapping of mountain trails not trodden since the ancient Celts made their way across country via uplands, the plains being covered with a dense growth of trees.

I, myself, do not power walk, greyhound follow, or road bowl wager. I walk for the curiosity and the uplift, the wonderments of the wayside and the 'high' of the free-flowing endorphins released after twenty minutes on the hoof. I am not so much a slow walker as one who is waylaid by the roadside attractions. Curiosity, atmosphere or amazement delays me, and while the company forges ahead, I am left behind, in thrall.

The walks outlined in this book are for walkers such as I. They take, generally, just a couple of hours but can easily be stretched to fill half a day. They are perfect for a weekend afternoon or a holiday meander.

They will, hopefully, stimulate my perambulating neighbours towards new horizons and inform visitors of the lovely land that awaits just off the tourist trail. I cannot imagine these local by-ways ever becoming crowded. We may in time meet a party of ardent Japanese, led by a person with a flag, or stout Austrians in lederhosen and braces singing "Falderee-Falderah". They will be sure of a welcome. We Irish delight in showing off our land.

To the farmers and landowners

But for the goodwill of farmers and landowners our chance to enjoy the landscape and wildlife of Ireland would be grievously curtailed. While nine tenths of the walks outlined in this book are on lanes and back roads, public routes do not always conveniently join up. To make circular routes, I have sometimes found old tracks, still in use. Local landowners, as elsewhere in West Cork, wish well to the walker but they quite reasonably point out that walkers crossing their property must accept that they do so at their own risk.

The area

Of the five areas now explored by this small series, this last, between Castletownshend and Sherkin, on the coast, and Skibbereen town, inland, is perhaps the most varied.

Skibbereen is the most typical of West Cork market towns. Disdaining the cosmopolitan flavour of Kinsale and the Celtic Tiger roar of Clonakilty, it is a comfortable, almost old fashioned place. Its customers are farmers, more than tourists. Its shops, well stocked and diverse, are unpretentious and homely. Many are still small businesses, where the customer is served by a family member summoned from the living quarters at the sound of the bell. It is a town replete with history, particularly the sad history of the Famine, with much to be seen by the student of those tragic years.

Contrast bustling, vernacular Skibbereen with Castletownshend, an enclave of a self appointed Anglo Irish ascendancy, a village unlike any other in Ireland, once peopled by excentrics, literary geniuses and officer soldiers who travelled to the ends of an empire upon which the sun then never set.

It is a lovely village, of fine Georgian houses, with a beautiful C of I church in the grounds of which lie buried Edith Somerville and Violet Martin, authors of Victorian/Edwardian classics. The village, on a steep slope, ends at the castle and the sea. There are still summer regattas. One can almost imagine the ghosts of bygone tennis parties coming to life and asking "Is there honey still for tea?".

There is ancient history there too - the best preserved ring fort in West Cork, and standing stones, stark and dramatic on the hills. Nature is bountiful, and on these walks, we especially encounter the flora and fauna of the seashore.

The routes described are three on land and two on islands. The islands are easily reached, one by a causeway, one by a short ferry ride. Historic Baltimore, gateway to the islands, is a classic small fishing and yachting port set on the shores of Roaring Water Bay. Beyond the restaurants, pubs, hotels and hostels, there are headlands as wild as any in Ireland, looking out over the broad Atlantic and the hundred islands of the bay.

At Ringarogy Island, on the mudflats and islets beside The Lag causeway, most wading birds species of these western shores can be seen. Nature is undisturbed. The farms are small, with rocky outcrops covered in gorse and heather between the small fields. We walk traffic-less lanes, in an island peace.

On Sherkin Island, the ruins of an ancient abbey greets us when we step off the 15 minute ferry from Baltimore Pier. We are, indeed, in another world, in another time. A ruined O'Driscoll castle looks across at the mainland; ancient culinary plants still grown on the castle walls. The narrow lanes take us to fine sandy coves, safe for swimming, to close views of Clear Island, and to island pubs where we may watch the sun sink before taking the last boat home.

Acknowledgements

I am indebted to the following for the kind assistance they gave me in researching this book.

- Norma Hurley, re. Ringarogy Island
- Matt Murphy, re. Sherkin Island
- Hideko Saito, re. wild flowers.
- Marie Enright, planning the routes.

Sources

- Archaeological Inventory West Cork Government Publications 1992
- The Coast of West Cork. Somerville Large, Appletree Press 1991
- Timoleague and Barryroe. James Coombes, local publication
- Lewis' Topographical Dictionary of Cork 1837. Collins Press 1998
- Sherkin Island. Dolly O'Reilly, local publication
- Islands of Ireland. Ritsema. Collins Press 1999
- West Cork. Brehony, Kestrel Books 1997
- Irish Birds. David Cabot, HarperCollins 1995
- Birds of Europe. Jonsson, Helm 1999
- The Wild Plants of Sherkin, Cape Clear and adjacent islands of West Cork. John Akeroyd, Sherkin Island Marine Station 1996
- Seashells and Seaweeds. Phillips. Elm Tree Books
- Seashore of Britain and Northern Europe, HarperCollins 1996
- Irish Herbal Cures. Scallan, Gill & Macmillan 1994
- British Birds, their folklore. Greenoak Helm1997
- Wild plants of the Burren. Nelson, Collins Press 1999

Castletownshend and Castlehaven

Unusual village, Bronze Age fort, literary graves, wild places.

Locality: OS Sheet 88, starting at 170315, Castlehaven School on the R596, 31 miles south east of Skibbereen.

Description and Distance: A loop walk, with 'spur' routes, $4^{1}/_{2}$ or $6^{1}/_{2}$ miles.

Walking Time: 3 or 4 hours.

Walking conditions: Almost all metalled byroads. Two sets of steep steps, and two steep roads. These are not essential to the 'loop', but the diversions are well worthwhile.

Features: So much human history that natural history must be sidelined. Neolithic forts, ruined and preserved churches, elegant Georgian houses, a unique Anglo Irish enclave, picturesque coasts and hidden strands.

Flora and fauna: The flora of stone walls, road verges. Some fauna of the sea shore.

Equipment: Comfortable shoes.

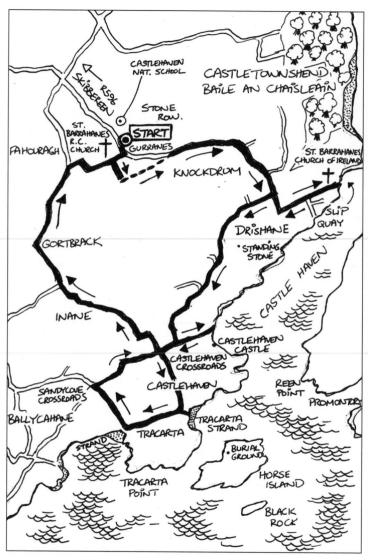

Castletownshend Walk

Itinerary:

(1) We begin at the car park opposite the fine, plain St Barrahane's RC church, about a mile before Castletownshend on the R596 Skibbereen-Castletownshend road. Hitching rings for mass-goers horses are set in the stone wall. The long stone building with the pink gable just up the road is Castlehaven National school, built in 1889; the derelict opposite is the old village hall.

The fields opposite the church are like rivers of green grass pouring down the hill, with islets of rock and gorse dividing them. These rise to gorse covered outcrops on the skyline. Three thin pillars are silhouetted against the sky, more like tall fence posts than pillars of stone. The remains of a stone row, they are dramatic on our left as we walk down the road. The big electricity poles and wires between us and them are unfortunate; perhaps, one day, the cables will be buried.

A stream runs below the church, with breaks of alder and a small marsh. The road is in a boggy dip; spike rushes edge the verge. Above the bend ahead, a flight of walled, stone steps climbs the slope on the other side of a field. We take the right turning before the bend, pass some houses and then take the first left. We pass a solitary house - once the schoolmaster's - and find a narrow path to the left about 100 yards beyond. This was the old road. It is somewhat overgrown - indeed, given that it leads walkers more safely than along the main road to one of the finest stone forts in West Cork, it would be sensible for the custodians of same to maintain this path. The ditches on either side support a host of maidenhair ferns, hard ferns, hart's tongue, polypody, wall rue, club moss and lichens. The polypody leaves are three times as long as they are wide, triangular from base to tip, with 'teeth' like a band saw. In spring, they have tiny, orange 'buttons' on the backs - the spores - laid out in twin lines, perfect and beautiful. Take a leaf home and dry it - polypodys are under no threat, they grow everywhere, on walls, rocks and trees.

We reach the steps; above, the round shape of the low fortress walls can be seen against the skyline. The steps are thoughtfully made, with a landing every so often; they are some 80 steps in all. At the top, we pass an iron wicket and a piece of field, and arrive at the fort.

(2) One is immediately taken by the view. Ahead and below, we have a 180° panorama of sky, sea and islands, behind, 180° of undulating landscape, ris-

*The Old Community Centre
opposite Castlehaven
National School*

ing to blue, distant hills. There can be few finer lookouts in Munster; on a clear day, we can see as far as Hungry Hill at Bantry, and the Macgillicuddy Reeks near Killarney.

Knockdrum, as the fort is called, is a national monument. Bronze Age, perhaps 3,000 to 4,000 years old, it was part-rebuilt in the mid 19th century and is wonderfully preserved; there are five other ring forts in the encompass of this walk but none compare. Boyle Somerville excavated and wrote on it in the 1930s. The walls, over five foot high, are eight feet across and provide a walkway around the perimeter which is all of twenty paces in interior diameter and unbroken but for the entrance, at which there is a low 'sentry house'. Inside, is a hut site, without a roof, and a souterrain tunnelled into the bedrock. It is said that Knockdrum was used through the ages as a lookout point for invaders. What a perch!

Below, is a small, brown lake, beyond it, the cliffs and Horse Island, flat, with a beach facing the mainland, cliffs at one end, fields divided by stone walls, a ruined house and sheep grazing. To the east, the entrance to Castlehaven Bay, with a white beacon marking Reen Point on the eastern shore. Over the back of Reen, we can see Blind Harbour, the causeway to Myross and the trapped water between it and Squince Harbour, a sea lake. Offshore, is Seal Rock, Low Island and then High Island, with a crescent of impressive cliffs. The headland in the distance is Galley Head, with lighthouse; the western headland is Scullane Point.

Outside the wicket, lies a recumbent rock, decorated with cup marks. These sometimes appear on standing stones. Their significance is elusive; they may have been miners' marks, astronomical coda, plans for hut settlements or doodles.

At the bottom of the steps, we pick up the old road again and walk east. The three standing stones are now closer, stark against the sky above the left slope. We reach the R596 road at a gate - in spring, a wood pigeon nests in the ash tree beside it - and a finger post indicating the fort. Opposite, is a gate, with a "no duty of care" notice on it; the land owner kindly hasn't said "No Entry" but is justifiably protecting himself against injury claims. I can give no directions and no encouragement to trespassers. Clearly, walkers do sometimes cross the field to view the Three Fingers, as the stones are called. Gorse and boggy ground intervene.

The stone row, viewed from the south, stands tall and thin on the hill's saddle against a near and far landscape of bog, pine plantation, rough land and mountain. Unfortunately, a large house is now in construction a mile away but dead centre in the view. When we think of standing stones, we think of robust items the height of cow scratching-posts in a pasture. These are more like 'pillar' stones, or even drunken telegraph poles when seen from afar. On close view, they prove to be grey columns, patterned with lichen. Two are over twelve feet tall, with another, fallen, about the same. I have no idea how big was the stone purloined by a 19th century Madam Townsend (according to Peter Somerville Large, a native of Castletownshend and author of a lapidary volume on West Cork). This stone, number five, should surely be resurrected from the undergrowth of Castletownshend castle gardens and replaced, flat or upright, on the hill. What a monument they are, that they should have stood for, perhaps, 4000 years, aligned with the sun rising on midsummer day.

(3) To reach Castletownshend village, the next attraction on our itinerary, we have no option but to use the main road. Once we reach the village, we have the safety of broad pavements.

After the village name plaque, a high stone wall on the left bounds the castle estate. The small cottages, opposite, were the habitations of the Irish, situated outside the village proper, as was the Catholic church, a mile back. Castletownshend was a unique Protestant, Anglo Irish village, an enclave of the ascendancy, with the wild Irish all around. Cradle of a self-appointed

West Cork 'gentry', through the ages it cultivated a genteel rapacity along with the English traditions of huntin', shootin' and fishin', and "is-there-honey-still-for-tea?"

The village street, descending from the impressive gates of an estate which once included a donkey sanctuary, is immediately striking and like no other in Ireland. Small cottages, once homes of the Irish and now painted in gay West Cork colours, give way to the stolid Georgian houses built by the Anglos further down. There are attractive oddities, "Fuschia", like a twee Olde English cottage, and Sundial House, with its dial over the door, tall chimney, and brick corniced windows. The 'flower pot', as it is known, stands in mid street, two sizeable trees growing out of it. There is a lovely Georgian house on the left and 'the billiard room' - as it once was - on the right. After Mary Ann's pub, with its various 'Good Food' recommendations, elegant townhouses line the pavements all the way down to the Townshends' Gothic pile.

The castle, built on the site of an older castle burnt down in 1856, now functions as a private residence and guest house. The grounds, well treed with some exotics, are private, and run down to the sheltered bay. A Colonel Richard Townsend received large grants of land here from the English parliament under the Act of Settlement 1652. The spelling of the name seems appropriate, considering that they did, in fact, live at the end of the town. However, this was later changed to Townshend, like the ennobled Townshends in England.

With the castle gate on the left, we take the lane down to the pier; old warehouses are being renovated as holiday homes on the right and, on the pier, the old granary is soon to become apartments. The pier is colourful, and busy in summer, with yachts and regattas. On the opposite shore is Reen Quay; further up, a pebble shoal and the impressive ruins of Raheen, an O'Donovan castle.

A boat slip runs down onto a pebble beach and, on the rocks, acorn barnacles thrive by the million, small miracles of nature often unnoticed. White, conical and outwardly like tiny limpets, they feed quite differently. As the tide covers them, the apex of the shell opens, allowing tiny 'fingers' to extend and trawl for plankton. Limpets graze; barnacles 'filter'.

*St Barrahane's
Church Of Ireland (winter)*

Many seaweeds cover these and local rocks, each with its special zone between low and high water, although zones overlap. Bladder wrack, at mid tide level, has two or three air bladders arranged on each side of the midrib; these 'pop' and provide entertainment for children when stamped on. The bubbles float the fronds to the surface for photosynthesis when the tide comes in. The fruiting bodies at the tips have 'goose pimples' which exude a sticky, bright ochre fluid.

Sugar kelp, long and thin, with frilly edges is often found washed up here. When dried, the fronds have a white 'icing sugar' deposit, much enjoyed in China and Japan. Amateur weather forecasters use it to gauge humidity.

On the way back up to the village, we pass a fine house which apparently belongs to a dog - "Prince's House", the sign says, with a portrait of the owner, a collie.

Again passing the castle gates, we turn right up a cloister-like lane, with the Townshend walls on our right, hung with red, or 'spur' valerian from May onward, a lovely garden escapee now common on old town walls, even in Cork city. A sign announces St Barrahane's Church of Ireland, with a fine hexagonal stone tower just ahead. Glen Barrahane was the old name for this whole valley, called after a native saint. It was later pronounced and written Castlehaven by the English and finally was named after its most important family.

Wide steps climb to the church, with an iron arch overhead and a yew tree on each side. Headstones of parishioners stand randomly about the well kept grounds, shaded by Scots pine and ti palms, and bright with orange montbretia and the spiked white flowers of New Zealand liberti in summer. Names recur, hyphenated to enshrine the family connections, for the small population of settlers intermarried constantly. Unusually for a C of I place of worship, the church is open to the public. I am sure this gesture is greatly appreciated by its many visitors.

It is a lovely church, shining and polished, with a patina of time and an ambience of solid sanctity and patriotism. Patriotism to Britain, of course; the walls bear plaques attesting to the gallantry of Castletownshend officers (they are all officers) in foreign battles, the famous Coghill who won the Victoria Cross defending the regimental colours against 30-to-1 odds in the Zulu Wars, Bushe of the Bombay Army, Colonel John Townsend who served with distinction in Portugal, Spain and France. A huge, perhaps vainglorious, marble tablet in a nave commemorates the history of the Townshend family while, in the church proper, more famous than any of CT's famous sons, her famous daughters, Edith Œnone Somerville and her cousin and collaborator, Violet Florence Martin (Martin Ross), authors of Some Experiences of an Irish RM (1899), are remembered in a plaque erected by American admirers. Their simple graves lie side by side behind the church, two Irish yews over them, the sea below.

Also recorded are the names of past parish rectors. One is surprised to find that the first few are O'Driscolls (1403) and O'Callaghan, but these were pre-Reformation, ministering at the ruined

The Three Fingers, with fallen stones

16

Knockdrum Ring Fort and Horse Island

church at Castlehaven, visited later on this walk. Post Reformation, the list abruptly changes to a litany of Anglo Saxon patronymics.

The ambient light in the church has an ecclesiastical glow, filtered through stained glass windows, reflecting on dark tiled floors and polished benches. Three of the windows are by Harry Clarke (1899 to 1931), premier stained glass artist of his time and reflect the art nouveau influence of Beardley and Arthur Rackham.   One depicts St Patrick and St George looking at one another across the Irish Sea.

(4) The village is a cul de sac; to leave it we must return the way we came, uphill and sharp right, past the walls of the Somerville's Drishane House on the left and taking the left turning, signed "Tragumna 10km".   The 'Coast Road', as it is called, is well treed, the ditches resplendent with primroses in April, flag iris - the French fleur-de-lys - in May, foxgloves in June, navel-wort in July, montbretia in August, sometimes - due to micro-climates and Gulf Stream vagaries - the whole lot blooming at once.   We pass a roadside well at a house entrance, on the right. Prehistory is in the fields all about us, a ringfort to the right, cromlechs, standing stones and cup-marked stones on the left. We have close views of Horse Island and soon take a sharp left down to Castlehaven Castle, the most of a mile there and back, but worth-while.

The road goes very steeply down, with dramatic views of the islands, to an apron above the pebble beach. In front, the sea; behind, an ancient grave-yard and Glenbarahane Church, already in ruins in 1615 - the parish church had become St. Barahane's in Castletownshend. Beyond it, on the shore, is a holy well. The church is reduced to a single gable; inside it, fuschia grows luxuriantly within the railings of an old tomb. It is a lonely place. The headstones are mainly stumps of weathered rock, with a few memorials as late at the 1970s, one even blanketed in artificial flowers. Snowdrops bloom here in January, once, no doubt, planted, now growing wild.

As we look out to sea, the ruins of Castlehaven Castle which, literally, col-lapsed in 1924, are on the 'cliff' on our right. It is barely detectable, ivy cov-ered and low. Dean Swift stayed there on a visit from Dublin in 1735. Once it was as grand as Raheen Castle, aforementioned; now it might be the ruins of a peasant bothán. I once met some treasure seekers with metal detectors nearby, inspired by a local farmer's tales of ploughed-up artefacts. They had found a few embossed buttons, defaced by time, shards of lead glazed pot-tery and a few flattened lead shot. In the bay offshore, a sea battle once raged, and the castle, which the O'Driscolls had ceded to their Spanish allies, was a target for the English guns.

In 1601, in what was to be the last stand of the old Gaelic world, the Spanish fleet arrived in Kinsale Harbour and waited for the armies of O'Neill and O'Donnell to march south. Six transport vessels of munitions and stores, under Don Pedro de Zuibar, were dispatched to here, Castlehaven Bay. An English convoy, under Admiral Sir Richard Leveson, sailed after them and attacked them in the bay, sinking four of the ill-armed galleons and firing on the castle, given over to the Spaniards by the O'Driscolls. However, Irish reinforcements arrived from the west in the form of Donal O'Sullivan Beare and five hundred men. De Zuibar took heart and, landing cannon at Reen Point, raked the English fleet which, trapped by a sudden west wind blow-ing in the harbour mouth, became easy targets for the Spanish guns.

According to some accounts, 500 English were slain before Leveson escaped. However, on Christmas Eve, 1601, the English had their revenge at the Battle of Kinsale, their victory over Gael and Spaniard heralding the final subjugation of Ireland and the arrival of planters and 'undertakers', Castletownshends et al, granted 'patents' for Irish lands.

The "Flower Pot" in the middle of the street

(5) The walk back up the glen to the main road is wooded and steep. Bird watchers might watch out for sparrowhawks, which are sometimes seen here. At the main road, we turn left, heading west to walk the 'square' touching Tracarta Strand and Sandy Cove. At Castlehaven Cross Roads, the footsore may take the road straight ahead over the hill for a shorter way home. After completing the square, the longer itinerary also uses this road and details will be found at paragraph (6), ahead.

A hundred yards east of the cross-roads, we turn left towards the sea. The high cliffs before Scullane Point are across the water to our right and, ahead, Horse Island, with a round tower erected to mark Castlehaven harbour. A side road left leads down to Tracarta Strand, a pebble beach, with two idyllic houses, with many flowers. Blue lesser periwinkle is in bloom in January, and lily, forget-me-not and montbretia has rooted almost on the sand. A friend told me that he once found the giant seed of a tree native to the Amazon Basin on this beach; it had floated down the river and across the Atlantic to Tracarta, Carthy's Strand. There are black and white oystercatchers, with red bills, out on the rocks, and many gulls.

The boathouse and Seafield House from the pier

We return to the main road and, walking west, enjoy wonderful views over the big bay between us and Scullane, white water beating the black cliffs in winter, mirror-calm and painted red by the sun setting of a summer evening. At the corner, Sandy Cove, a small, white beach lies below us, reached by many steps. One wild February 14th, standing on the rain-blown cliff above I read "Happy Valentine's Day, Anne" written on the sand. Not a soul was to be seen in the landscape. Would Anne come in out of the sea?

(6) We walk north from the cove and, at Sandycove Cross Roads, turn right. The road is largely straight, and pleasant, with much fuschia in the hedges and little traffic.

After a half mile, we are back at Castlehaven Cross Roads, where we turn left, climbing steadily up a rain runelled road to about 120m, with fine views to the north and to Flea and Horse islands, south. Prehistory is, again, close by, a ringfort to the right, and modern, somewhat tragic, history, a 'cillín', to the left. Here, unbaptised children were buried; also suicides and the unidentified dead.

We bear right at the two "Y" junctions we meet. Shortly, Knockdrum can been seen atop the hill, and we are back on the R596, in front of the school.

Skibbereen town and Abbeystrowry

An old West Cork market town on a lovely river, with a nearby abbey and famine graveyard.

Locality: OS Sheet 89. We start at 123336, in the centre of the town.

Description and Distance: A loop of $4^1/2$ miles, much of it along a traditional Skibbereen walk, "The Compass Ring".

Walking Time: $2^1/2$ hours.

Walking conditions: All metalled byroads. Two short climbs.

Features: An old style market town. The Ilen River. Abbeystrowry Abbey, and dramatic famine memorials.

Flora and fauna: Plants of cliff faces and humid places. Gorse-covered hillsides and river banks. Old walls festooned in valerian and buddleia. River birds - herons, ducks, cormorants.

Equipment: Comfortable shoes.

Itinerary:
(1) Our starting point is the Maid of Eireann statue outside the Town Hall. The statue, erected by Young Irelanders in 1904, once stood more centrally as a traffic island but was so often clipped by trucks that it was decided to move it before it was irrevocably damaged. Where it now stands, the inscriptions on the four faces of the limestone base can be less hazardously read. The plaques records four glorious risings in Ireland's fight for freedom, 1798 (Wolfe Tone, the Protestant United Irishman), 1803 (Robert Emmet and the Young Irelanders), 1848 (Davis, Duffy et al) and 1867 (The Fenians). Ireland's sad and gallant history is recorded on the plinth below the Maid.

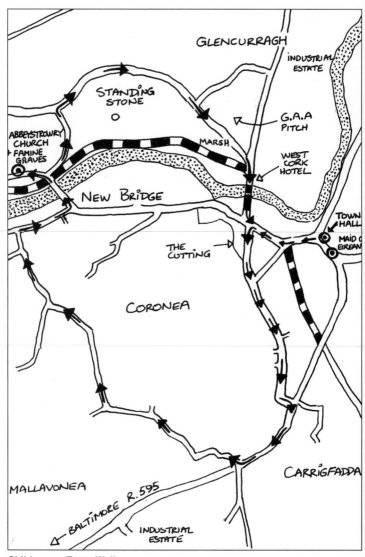

Skibbereen Town Walk

The Town Hall, built 1863, is alongside, with the Skibb. coat of arms over the door, "Quod petis hic est..." (What you seek is here). Classical plays and light entertainments are regularly staged within. We set off down Main Street, staying on the left pavement; we will use the opposite pavement for our return.

Skibbereen is, arguably, the most 'typical' of West Cork market towns. The centre has changed little in seventy years. Main Street has some double shop fronts at first, the prosperous, sensible retailers one would expect in a busy country town. The exteriors are pleasantly old fashioned, but the goods for sale are modern and sophisticated.

Further down, at The Square where the Caol Stream flows under the road to join the Ilen, Main Street becomes Bridge Street and the businesses are mainly small shops. A feature of the shop windows is an external horizontal bar designed to stop loafers of a more leisurely age taking up a perch on the window sill, or passing cows or horses from knocking in the glass on Fair Days.

The Caol runs beside the car park entrance, a healthy little stream despite its journey through the town. It is overhung by buddleia, flowering purple in late summer, a favourite of butterflies. It, like the red valerian that festoons the town's old walls, will grow almost anywhere. Mallard and hybrid farmyard ducks paddle in the Caol waters, an otter is regularly seen and a johnny-the-bogs, - a.k.a the grey heron - fishes on the bank and nests on a tall tree above North Street.

Beyond the car park, is a small, red brick Methodist Church, and then the gates to the town's weekly Livestock Mart and Country Market. Alongside, is Abbeystrewery C of I church, with an impressive arched gate in memory of an ex-rector, James Goodman, a pro-

Goodman Memorial Gate, Skibbereen

Then "New" Bridge on the Illen, looking towards Skibbereen

fessor of Erse at Trinity College, Dublin, and an uilean piper who collected and preserved 2,000 uilean airs. Sited on the cloistered grounds is the old school and Community Hall, with the date 1907 over the door.

To walk down Bridge Street, especially when the small shops are lit in the evening, is to take a trip down Memory Lane. Most West Cork towns still have a few 'cottage' businesses; nowhere are there so many as in Skibb. "Hucksters' shops", they were once called, but not pejoratively. Family retailers, their profusion and proportions provided opportunity for a variety of social exchange before the advent of self-service. There is little advertising and the windows display only a token of the stock; the name over the door is sufficient endorsement of the product. When the door bell dings, a family member appears. Goods are plain, transactions unhurried. Every staff of life and leisure is available, milk, bread, eggs, fags, The Examiner, The Star and penny sweets. Happily, these shops have changed little and add a charming character to the town.

(2) At a pub on a corner called Baby Hanna's, we turn sharp left. Above us, on the gable, is painted a huge locomotive steaming at a station; the street ahead was the old railway line which, before closure in 1961, carried trippers west to Baltimore, and fish east to Cork. The Cutting - so it is called - is a sort of Hanging Gardens of Skibbereen, a chasm almost Amazonian in ambience, green, wet, glistening and exotic. A dozen varieties of wild fern

24

and succulents root on the rock walls, down which small or, sometimes, rain-swollen, freshets flow. For the botanist, fine examples of plants found on mortared or dry stone walls are here seen in their natural habitat, rooting on plain rock. Spleenwort, for instance, a small elegant fern with leaves like beadlets along a 'horsehair' stem, is especially robust, and maidenhair fern, cultivated as a house plant, thrives in the misty air.

Emerging from the man-made gorge, we pass the back of the Mart and the top of Mardyke Street; a garden centre is on the slope above. Keeping left, we arrive at the main Skibb-Baltimore R595 road. Here, we turn right and, after a few hundred yards, turn right again up a steep road signposted "Marguerite's B&B". This quiet byway, weaving uphill before reaching the highest point, Ardsolus ("high light") is part of The Compass Ring, a time-honoured Skibbereen promenade. There are good views south to Lick Hill, between us and the sea, about three miles away as the crow flies. To the north, are the high hills behind Drimoleague, twelve miles distant. Topping the rise, we descend to the Ilen valley.

(3) At the river, we turn right, along its bank. The Ilen is tidal up to Skibbereen and, until relatively recent times, women would row here to the corn mill and market from the islands of Roaring Water Bay. Doughty oars-women, they came from as far away as Long Island, off Schull. Skibbereen is said to have been founded by English settlers who came inland up the river from Baltimore after Algerian pirates raided that coastal town in 1631 and carried off 110 of their number.

Translated as 'the glittering water', the Ilen was a fine salmon river, providing a living to local families until equipment became so sophisticated and nets-men so numerous that stocks could not be sustained. Referring to the wholesale slaughter, the salmon were said to "come up by river and go back by road..."

Abbeystrowry. The gate to the famine graves

Along the Ilen, cormorants fish, and herons. Dippers are common on the upper reaches, like large, white-breasted robins that have the knack of walking along the stream bottom winkling crustacea from under stones. As we cross the bridge in early summer, the line of flaming gorse over the water towards Skibbereen is so breathtaking that I can never resist a photo. I never do the scene justice and, no doubt, never shall.

The 'New Bridge', so called - it was built in 1826 - is a fine, stone edifice, with five arches, edged with a lighter shade of limestone. When the tide is up, perfect circles are reflected on the water beneath; bats roost in the darkness, and skim the water at twilight. Crossing it, and the main N71 road to Ballydehob, we head up the lane opposite, but divert west a few hundred yards to find the gate into the graveyard and ruined church of Abbeystrowry.

(4) The great tragedy that befell Skibbereen in the black '48 - and in the black 1846, and 1847 - a tragedy that seems to eclipse that of any other town in Ireland, is here evidenced in the famine graves. Skibbereen suffered devastation in the Great Famine. The population halved. The streets were crowded with the dying destitute from all over West Cork and the workhouse was so inundated that those allowed in for soup were too numerous to be easily removed. Working men, flocking to the town in search of famine relief work at 6p a day, died of starvation not having received their wages for six days. Protestant landowners formed a fund to provide soup and, by contribution of 1/9d per month, received chits for 4 litres of soup daily which they

Fuschia flower

then distributed to those they thought most in need. Meanwhile, grain, vegetables and other produce continued to arrive in the town from inland and was shipped from the Ilen quays to Cork to be exported to Britain and America. Trevelyan, of the British Treasury, decreed that this food should not be made available free for the dying Irish. Just as in the case of Third World hand-outs today, the maintenance of 'market forces' was paramount and took precedence over the sustenance of life.

Here, in the Abbey graveyard, is a plot where some 9,000 famine dead were buried,

Grey Heron on the River Illen

sawdust scattered over them for want of coffins. Five limestone slabs, standing near a roofed gate where there was once a keeper's cottage, commemorate them poignantly in poetry and prose - "Oh, God, that bread should be so dear, and human flesh so cheap!".

Other plaques commemorate the founder of the Sisters of Charity in the USA and the Manchester Martyrs, Irish republicans executed at Salford Jail in 1867. Near the ruins of the abbey itself, a naive but emotive monument, a white painted iron cross, with harp, was wrought by a local blacksmith in memory of the famine dead.

Of the church, originating on the site of a monkish cell, little remains. "The only daughter" of the Cistercian Church, circa 1270, at Abbeymahon on Courtmacsherry Bay, (ref. Fr. James Coombes), it is gone but for an ivy clad east gable and parts of the north and south walls. It was 'in repair' in 1695, in 'bad repair' in 1806; it was replaced, in 1827, by a church which became the present cathedral.

(5) Returning, through the wicket, onto the 'top' road, we retrace our steps to the junction above the bridge and turn left, uphill. This is a pleasant, very quite road, with houses with fine gardens and views. Below, to the right, the Ilen winds out of Skibb., golden between dark banks when the sun is from the west. The town is laid out, a mile or so ahead, the cathedral dwarfing the buildings all around.

At the T junction, we turn right. We are now on the 'high' road arriving in Skibbereen from Turkhead, Pig's Bridge and points west; the lower road, the N71, runs along the Ilen. Between the roads, are two ringforts and a standing stone, the edge of one fort visible from the road, a slight undulation with some sceacs or whitethorns. Ringforts are everywhere in Ireland, and this site is typical of the hill-shoulder locations favoured in West Cork. They were, in fact, enclosed farmsteads, built in early Christian times, the purpose of the surrounding bank being to keep out predators like wolves or cattle-thieving neighbours. The standing stone is, apparently, still standing but near others which have fallen.

Wayside foxgloves in June

We reach the low ground at the 30mph speed-limit sign at the edge of town. There is a stout stone barn on our left and, on the right, fields between us and the N71 which are inundated with Ilen water at spring tides; the cattle stand knee deep, or on knolls, waiting for the tide to go out. Then, on the left, is the GAA pitch and a big cut stone gate topped by a statue of local revolutionary, Jeremiah O'Donovan Rossa, silhouetted against the sky. Inside, a memorial park to O'D R is in construction at the time of writing.

(6) Reaching the T junction, we turn right and cross the Ilen via Kennedy Bridge, commemorating JFK, whose ancestors came from Abbey, a mile downriver. Behind it, is the old metal railway bridge - the line ran through the site of the, now, ballroom of the West Cork Hotel, the adjacent hostelry with fine colonial-style balcony bringing a touch of old New Orleans to Skibbereen. Across the road is a more sombre presence, a fine old stone building in decayed condition, four storeys with three rows of six windows over the river, four rows of three windows over the street. This was the Steam Mill, built pre-Famine for grinding grain; now a bicycle shop occupies the ground floor. Here, in 1845, the famished citizenry in its rags - all else being pawned - queued for soup or died on the pavement, or on the Ilen banks nearby.

A hundred yards further, on the left, is the office of the Southern Star. For some years, the population of Skibbereen suffered a dearth of newsprint, with the Skibbereen Eagle, virulently Unionist and anti-Irish, besieged by the 'new' Southern Star, Catholic, nationalist and regularly banned by the authorities. The Eagle was an eccentric weekly and published the oft-quoted editorial warning the Czar of all the Russias that The Skibbereen Eagle was keeping its eye on his goings-on. In 1929, it was finally eclipsed by The Star.

We turn the corner, left, at the T junction and take the left pavement of Bridge Street and, then, Main Street to return to the Maid of Eireann. En route, we pass The Eldon Hotel, where the Free Stater, General Michael Collins, had his last meal before departing to meet his undeserved fate at Beal na Blath, the Mouth of Flowers, where he was gunned down by the IRA.

(7) A little further down the historic thoroughfare, we pass O Leary's retailers, the gable of which proudly bears a fresco of the handsome Jeremiah O' Donovan Rossa and a plaque describing him as "Founder of the Phoenix National and Literary Society, who traded in this shop 1853 to 1859". O'D R, proposing Ireland for the Irish, was quickly banged up in Mountjoy Goal by the British, along with his many Skibbereen adherents.

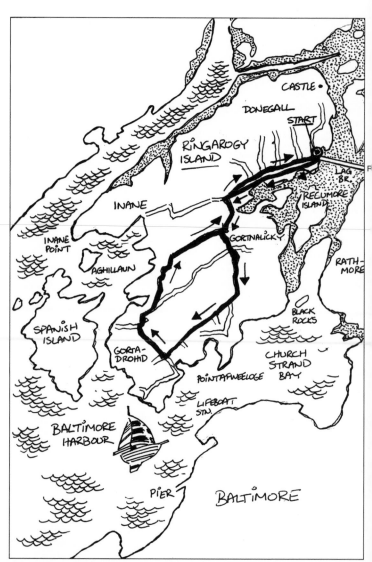

Ringarory Island Walk

Ringarogy Island

A gentler pace, country lanes, few cars, much nature.

Locality: OS Sheet 88, starting at 059292, the east end of Lag Bridge, just off the Skibbereen-Baltimore R595 road.

Description and Distance: A large circle and a narrow oval. The waist section joining the two is repeated. 4 miles.

Walking Time: 1¹/₂ hours, at a lively pace - but twice as long if one stops to admire the birds, flowers and islands.

Walking conditions: All metalled lanes. No steep climbs.

Features: The Ringarogy circuit is an education in Irish fauna and flora with its array of sea and wading birds for easy viewing, common and rare plants by the roadside, and panoramas of sea, islands and sky.

Flora and fauna: Trees and flowers of wetlands, roadside flowers, migrant and resident water birds.

Equipment: Comfortable shoes, and binoculars if possible.

Itinerary.
Ringarogy means "point of the small portion". This, perhaps, refers to the island, O'Driscoll territory, as a small portion of their extensive mainland demesnes.

In Ringarogy, the peace and quiet of another era still obtains. The houses may be modern or modernised but the roads are lanes and one rarely sees a car. There are few human artefacts to distract us from nature. The stones of the O'Driscoll castle that once stood at the north end were spirited off to build the cathedral at Skibbereen in 1826. A small cillín and perhaps a dozen houses are passed on the entire four mile route. Once, almost 800 people lived here; now, there are about 70. I can think of few more pleasant walks in West Cork.

(1)   We set off at the west side of the causeway known as the Lag Bridge. The Ilen washes the north west shore of Ringarogy. Here, on the north east side, The Lag is a silted up channel, filled and emptied by the tides, a 'lag' or area of low ground between mainland and island.

If the tide is out and it is winter, one is immediately arrested by the bird life. Out on the mudflats between the small islets and rocks, a dozen species stalk or waddle about, identifiable with the naked eye. If it is summer, there will be many less, but there will be some. If the tide is in, one should look out for birds on the shores; they will not be as easy to see but some colourful species - e.g. black-and-white oystercatchers, with bright red bills - will be obvious, and others will be roosting near them.

The most striking birds here are the shelduck, big as small geese, with glorious black-green heads, chestnut collars, pure white breasts and red legs and beaks.   They are present all year but are fewer in July and August when most adults fly to Heligoland, in the Baltic, or to the Bristol Channel, to moult, leaving their offspring in the care of a few crèche minders. When they return, parents and offspring recognise one another immediately, and reunite.

Shelduck nest in rabbit burrows, sometimes many miles from the sea whither the ducklings have to walk only days after hatching. A nine mile walk is on record so, should any of us humans flag on this short circuit, may we be inspired by the thought of waddling more than twice the distance on duckling legs. The shelduck do, in fact, eat shells - the tiny hydrobia snails which they hoover by the thousand off the mud flats have thin, whorled shells - but they are not called for that, rather for the old word "sheld" meaning variegated and referring to their colour. Colony nesters, the drakes may fight over favourite abandoned rabbit warrens.   A duck that does not find a nest may become a 'cuckoo

Flag Iris, the Fleur-de-lys of France

The Lag Bridge, just off the R595

female', surreptitiously laying once or even twice in another's nest. As shelducks lay an average of eleven eggs, the unfortunate nest-mother may find herself incubating some thirty three hatchlings; this has been recorded, and all survived. I would be fascinated to meet such a brood on its way to the water.

Out on the slob, redshank, greenshank, curlew and oystercatchers stalk insects and worms; a cubic metre of healthy estuary mud is said to contain more life than a cubic metre of Amazon top soil. The redshank's call will be one of the first sounds heard, clear, fluting notes - tu-ee, tu-ee, tu-ee - redolent of wildness and loneliness. Ever wary, it rises as we pass, a thin, brown wader, known in flight by its white wing edges, white rump and tail, and red legs trailing. It bobs and ducks as it struts about the shallows, much more nervous that its cousin, the greenshank (green legs, taller and whiter, and a white V up its back as it flies) which is generally seen alone. Some 500 greenshank cross from Scotland to Ireland in winter, while redshank, including Iceland immigrants, may number 25,000. About 5,000 redshanks breed here, on lake shores and in the Shannon callows, last stronghold of the corncrake.

Channelled wrack, a short seaweed, thrives on the rocks along the edge of the causeway. It forms a distinct belt, defining the upper level of the tides.

It has no 'bubbles' but can hold water in the 'channels' of the fronds and so avoid desiccation when tide levels fall for a few days.

We walk south west. Gorse and heather skirts the lane; the trees we will encounter, apart from a few pines, are sallies, goat willow and alder. The sally bushes bear furry buds in spring; the alders have catkins and small cones. The gorse is French Gorse, spring flowering and up to six foot high, and Dwarf Gorse which flowers in autumn, with the heather. Gorse seeds from Ireland were taken to Scotland and Wales to grow fodder for cattle. The islets and islands of the Lag and the bay are dressed twice a year in mantles of yellow, or yellow and purple. The shore-line rocks are splattered with white and orange lichens. The rocks are black, the sheltered waters dark, reflecting all these colours. Any wonder West Cork is one of the loveliest places on earth.

Lapwing or Peewit

As we hoof it along the road, away to the south east is the signal tower behind Baltimore and, nearby, we have new views of the slob, with silver or blue channels running between the mud, depending on the colour of the sky. Other ducks, red headed widgeon, with white wing bars, from Iceland, Scandinavia, Russia and Siberia, and tiny teal, some Irish, some Continental, frequent these secluded places. The teal drakes have a yellow spot near tail, and 'lacquered' red heads, with a green 'Chinese' eye, brilliant and exotic in sunlight.

Sedge edges the road for a few yards; streams inside and outside the road ditch are regular, with spike rush, water biswort and fools watercress thriving. A road merges from the right - we will be returning to the causeway along it. This area is Donegall West; the old name for the island is Dunnegal. There are rhododendron clumps here and there, green shrubs with shiny, leathery leaves. It has either been culled or has some natural restriction; it is an extremely invasive species in areas of high rainfall and acid soils, swallowing up huge tracts of land, wiping out all native, ground dwelling flora - but it does have glorious purple blooms in early spring.

(2) We branch left at a corner, ignoring the road straight ahead. Here, there is much honeysuckle on the ditch beneath a break of alders. Typically, the alders grow by a stream. A bit of quarry breaks the ground on the left, with spoil heaps covered with vegetation. On the right, we have examples of 'rivers of green', narrow fields running down to the road between rock and gorse grown outcrops. Around isolated houses are wind sculpted trees. Turning to look back, we enjoy great views over the slobs and channels of The Lag.

Shelduck

(3) The road divides in a "Y". We take the left branch. Shortly, there is a road right, diagonally crossing the circle we will walk. We ignore it. There are some fuschia hedges from here on and, on the roadside, blackthorn and whitethorn sceacs, their branches permed like windblown hair. As the road descends gently, we see Spanish Island and the mouth of the Ilen to the right, Turk Head and, far off, Mount Gabriel, behind Schull. There is a small pond on our left, full only in winter, when it sometimes hosts a pair of mallard duck. Soon, Baltimore is seen, with a line of holiday cottages below the O'Driscoll 'castle'. A fine farmhouse with a new roof is up a lane to the left and, beyond it, on the right, some stone outbuildings which, at the time of writing housed a white faced donkey. Montbretia edges both sides of the road, flaming orange in August, appropriately wild-looking in this location - although it is, in fact, a French nursery 'concoction', a garden escapee.

We pass a fuschia hedge and some escalonia - both stoutly withstand salt breezes - and, below some trees on the left, a house with attractive and unusual windows, and a turquoise roof on the porch. We soon find ourselves walking downhill, with the sea straight ahead. The vicious, black rocks below the Sherkin lighthouse, the white beacon on the Baltimore side and, then, the coloured houses of Baltimore come into view. The vista is large from here; Sherkin, the pier and the hinterland, Spanish Island and others.

Grey Crow (Hooded Crow in the UK) feasting on mussles

Ringarogy, while naturally welcoming, has the most "No trespassing" and "The owner excludes the duty of care" notices per mile of road I have ever seen. In fact, the Occupiers' Liability Act 1995 (Section 5) protects farmers from injury or damages claims by entrants. The walker is expected to exercise judgement. Farmers cannot be held responsible for the actions of fools. As we know, we should avoid livestock and crops, close gates, and leave nothing behind us and take nothing with us when we leave.

As we face Baltimore town, just before a ruin on the left, we swing sharp right, almost a hairpin. On the right of the road is a long line of alders, overhanging a robust little stream inside the ditch. They are spaced as if planted but this would be unusual - alders seed themselves along watercourses all over Europe, having small cones which float (they are the only deciduous cone-bearing tree). Alders thrive on wet land, fixing nitrogen with their roots, and improving it. The male catkins, and female-catkins-become-cones exist side by side, burgeoning larders for siskins, small yellow-black birds which flock on the trees in winter. The stand we are passing would keep a flock from October to March as the seeds slowly ripens; they take only the ripest and move from tree to tree, calling shrilly as they go. No siskins bred here until 100 years ago but Thompson, author of A Natural History of Ireland, 1849, knew them well, saying, "They fed wholly on the alder, and looked beautiful, hanging like little parrots, picking at the drooping seeds of that tree..."

Mosses and a beautiful crinkly grey lichen, tree lungwort, flourish on these mature trees. Lichens aren't one plant but a combination of organisms. Some lichens are edible, some contain antibiotics and some live for 10,000 years. Opposite, the stone wall is colonised with delicate maiden hair fern and, also, stout, spectacular foxgloves, four and five feet tall in a good year, covered in purple bells and a favourite of bumble bees. Honeysuckle also blooms profusely along this sheltered road.

We see the water again, ahead of us, and Mount Gabriel, far off. A perfect 'river of green' flows down to the road, with electricity poles marching up it. Two standing gables of a ruin stand starkly on a low hill to the west. Spanish Island is beyond - it can be reached at low tide - and, then, the sheltered inlet between us and the Ilen mouth. We ignore the road to the right,

Shelduck nest in old rabbit burrows

the south end of the 'diagonal'. The sea is now hidden by rising ground. There are big mussel shells on the road, dropped by grey crows from aloft and, once cracked, prized open. This crow, also called the hooded or scald crow, is indeed a handsome bird, with a grey mantle and a shiny black head, breast and wings. It mates for life, and nests low, often in windblown sceacs or stone walls. They are common in West Cork but a surprise to many English and European city dwellers who have never before seen them.

We pass a 'dream cottage' on a trimmed green lawn by the sea and now, there is wet ground on the left, with many bright flag irises blooming in June, Irish spurge and wispy, creamy, meadowsweet in August. Meadowsweet was once strewn on the earthen floors of farmhouses for its scent, and was the first source of aspirin, the world's most widely used drug. Its sleepy bouquet scents the air after a warm summer's day.

We arrive back at the full round of the circle, retrace our steps past the small quarry, and turn right at the T junction. We pass the rhododendron, and a road to the left, and then the road splits. We take the 'high' road, the left branch of the narrow 'Y'. We pass an old farmhouse, and modern houses in pastel colours, a house with boats on the lawn and, then "Reengaroga National School 1913" now converted to a fine dwelling house with dormers. In March, wild daffodils grow along here and this high road is a lovely walk of a summer evening when the western sun picks out the gold-and-purple of Recumore Island and the islets of The Lag, like jewels set in silver.

Just before we reach the causeway, a small break of goat willow stands over land which is flooded in winter. Brilliant green moss clothes the trunks and branches. One late winter afternoon, when we arrived here after a shower, bright beadlets of water hung from the buds, sparkling in the sun. Some poetic soul remembered the Austin Clarke line about "brightness drenching through the branches"; and, as new waves of haze swept in across the causeway, we thought of "the mist becoming rain".

Baltimore Town and Beacon

Cliffs, moor land, panoramic views of Roaring Water Bay.

Locality: OS Sheet 88, starting above Baltimore Pier, 045265

Description and Distance: A loop walk through historic Baltimore town and out onto the wild headlands to the west. About 3½ miles.

Walking Time: 2 hours.

Walking conditions: The walk begins and ends on roads but the middle third, to the beacon and along the cliffs, is not for the frail or fainthearted. There are steep climbs, and the going is sometimes rough, on narrow paths through gorse and heather. Parts may be muddy and slippery in winter.

Features: Historic fishing village, with houses perched above the harbour. The beacon and the coastal hills just west of the village afford wide views over the Atlantic and the islands of Roaring Water Bay. On many days, the wind is, itself, a feature, blowing from the south west off a thousand miles of ocean.

Flora and fauna: Coastal and moor land species. Lusitanian slugs, diverse sea birds. Often, seals.

Equipment: Stout boots in winter. Stout trousers - the gorse is prickly on the calves.

Itinerary:
(1) We begin outside the pubs and restaurants above the pier. Below us, parked on trolleys, dry-docked yachts and fishing boats await scraping, repair or refurbishing. It is a colourful scene; Baltimore is a classic fishing hamlet. From the stone jetty, ferries ply to Sherkin and Clear islands and summer ferries navigate "Carbery's Hundred Isles" to Schull, on the north shore of Roaring Water Bay.

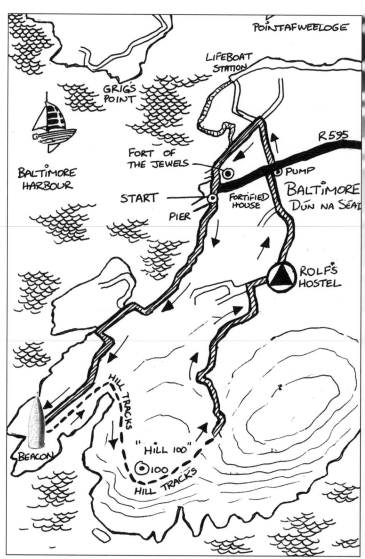

Baltimore Walk

The name, Baile an Tí Mór, the "town of the big house", probably refers to Dunashad Castle, the south gable of which rises high over the street to our right. The signpost gives Dun na Sead as the Irish name for Baltimore but this may owe more to the passion of gaelgóirí in the County Council than to historical accuracy. Dun Sead was the house but Baile an Tí Mór was the name of the town since it began. Disappointingly for Americans, Baltimore, Maryland has no connection.

Dunashad Castle, a traditional Irish tower house with 17th century refinements overlooking the harbour, was built by Fineen O'Driscoll on the site of an earlier castle, destroyed around 1540 by English settlers from Waterford in retaliation for the seizure of a cargo of wine by Fineen. For good measure, they also burnt the friary and villages on Sherkin, and the O'Driscoll fleet.

From early times, the O'Driscolls ruled West Cork between Kinsale town and the Kenmare River; later, O'Sullivans and O'Mahonys usurped much of their lands. The castles of the Baltimore O'Driscolls included Dunashad, the Fort of the Jewels, Dunalong, on Sherkin, the Fort of the Ships, Dunanoir, on Cape Clear, the Fort of Gold, Dunagall, on Ringarogy, and others.

Much O'Driscoll land was confiscated as punishment for joining the Geraldine Rebellion of 1534 but some was later restored and Fineen the Rover, for swearing allegiance to England and confiscating Spanish ships for the Crown, became Sir Fineen, High Sheriff of Cork, and was granted all the O'Driscoll lands as his personal property. His son left for Spain in disgust. However, Fineen sided with the Gaelic cause in 1601 and handed over castles to the Spaniards (see Castlehaven in Castletownshend Walk). His lands were again confiscated after the defeat at Kinsale. He was left with Baltimore town, which he leased to English settlers.

When Algerian corsairs sacked Baltimore on the night of June 20th, 1631, some 110 of these settlers were carried off to the slave markets and harems of the Barbary Coast. Subsequently, in fear, those remaining moved inland and founded the town of Skibbereen. Eighteen years later, an emissary from the English parliament sent to North Africa to ransom captives could find only two of the Baltimore slaves.

After the Great Famine devastated Baltimore in the black 1840s, a navigation school and boat building industry were set up by clergy and the gentry to assist in the recovery of the town. Salting and exporting mackerel was an industry of the entire West Cork coast in the late 1800s. It is said that in the early 1900s, some sixteen trainloads a day of fish left Baltimore for Cork, thence to be exported to America. All this ended when America imposed tariffs, but fishing and boats are still the lifeblood of Baltimore. The French are back too, with the French Glenans Sailing Centre on the pier.

Our walking route from the pier is via the main street, passing above the harbour. About half a mile west, we reach a pebble beach with a small promenade and some benches. The sheltered cove is popular for swimming in summer, and mackerel shoals sometimes sweep in, leaving the tideline silver with beached sprat. It is a pleasant spot from which to watch the sunset light up the painted houses of Baltimore. Birds sing all about - the gardens are popular with thrushes, blackbirds, robins and wrens. The promontory beyond the beach is the site of some fine houses, amongst pines.

(2) We leave the beach at the fingerpost indicating "The Beacon" and walk west, at first passing between houses. The house on the right, powder pink at the time of writing, is a typical farmhouse, little changed, with the traditional dormers under the roof. Once, it was probably the only house on this beach.

The road is narrow, and soon divides in a "Y". The right branch leads down to a small cove; we follow the left, walking slightly uphill. Birders should look out for newly arrived wheatears in March and April, restless birds, flying from rock to rock, bobbing and flicking, with a conspicuous white rump that marks them out from all other birds in this rocky landscape. They come from Africa to summer with us, although some continue as far as Iceland and Greenland. They nest in rock crevices or old rabbit burrows.

French Gorse, in flower

Much of the time, the pier on Sherkin Island and the road that winds up from it to the post office is straight ahead across the sound. We pass the 'last' house, with a weather vane in the

42

Baltimore, with the ruins of Fort of the Jewels

shape (it seems) of a sperm whale. Then, the last electricity post. We are now in wild, houseless country and the road climbs a slight rise towards the sky. On late Spring evenings, cock linnets, with their red breasts and crowns, sing amongst the tall gorse - French Gorse as it sometimes known - in the fields alongside; we will shortly encounter Irish or Western Gorse, a dwarf variety. When in bloom, gorse scents the air like coconut or vanilla, and the flowers make a strongly flavoured country wine.

The man-made roadside walls are a significant influence on the distribution of local flora. Splattered with lichens, mainly unmortared and often earth filled, they are colonised by the flora of rock outcrops and cliffs. Pennywort or navelwort is very common, so called because the soft, round leaves are the size of an old penny, with a 'navel' off-centre. Pretty hart's-tongue fern is everywhere at the wall footings, and primeval looking hard fern, shiny, with deep 'teeth'. Rusty back fern is an interesting species, seemingly withered and dead when dry but quickly reviving to a rich green in wet weather, with the undersides of the leaves covered in a rich, golden down.

Nearby, to left and right of the road, the land is bony with rock outcrops, carpeted with gorse and heather, bright in summer. Here and there on the hillside to the left, dry stone walls enclose irregular areas, one like a figure of

43

eight; mountain sheep were herded into such paddocks at shearing or dipping time. Now, they are overgrown with bracken, like the unfenced hill all around. The remains of a pilchard "pallace" is somewhere lost in the ferns and the briars.

This road leads only to the Beacon. Few cars pass on winter weekdays, rather more in summer. At weekends, whatever the weather, the Irish take their children to see this wonder of the western world. It looks like a rocket, gleaming white and pointing skyward. "Lot's Wife", it is called on old maps, comparing it to a pillar of salt. It was erected following English ner-

Sherkin Lighthouse from Baltimore Beacon

vousness after the failed French invasion at Bantry in 1796. Beacons and signal towers were built all along the coast, each within in sight of its neighbour to east and west. We will see one to the east of us when we top the hill.

(3) To reach the Beacon, one needs be in the full of one's health - the route is a steep climb from the car park below. Footholds are worn into the rock, uneven and slippery in winter. Beyond, the cliff falls away, sheer and precipitous.

A narrow strait divides this headland from Sherkin Island and its lighthouse and keeper's cottage close by. Black teeth of rocks show above the sea's surface on either shore, lashed with spray and white with froth when the strong south westerlies are blowing. The sea thunders in, and the wind howls. It is hard to imagine a more dramatic place to sit in the face of a western gale, watching the pounding waves and the grey storm clouds over the Atlantic. It is hard to imagine a more peaceful place to sit of a calm summer evening, with the sea blue below, the island across the water splashed with gorse and heather, and the big, white gannets diving on the mackerel near inshore.

The views over the sea world and islands are already panoramic and do not improve by being a few yards closer. Cliff top grass is shiny; a slip may mean tobogganing to oblivion on the seat of one's pants. The light over the Atlantic and the islands is often magical, the pearly clouds suffused by sunlight. Sometimes sunbeams, like searchlights, pan across Sherkin and the sea.

The nearby waters of the Celtic Sea were always the centre of a fishing industry, attracting boats from all over Europe, particularly France. As far back as the 15th century, pilchards were caught and pressed - in fish "pallaces" - for "train oil", used for lamps and in tanning leather. Later, when the huge shoals of pilchard mysteriously disappeared, vast harvests of mackerel and herring replaced them.

The spot height of the rise behind the Beacon is 44 metres. The scalp of the first hill east, beyond a narrow intervening cove, is our next destination, at a height of 100 metres above the sea.

(4) We descend to the cove by relatively clear, foot-worn paths over sparsely vegetated rock, and walk along its northern rim. A cave, with a square 'lintel', bores into the hillside above the shale beach. Grey seals are seen in this cove; greys are common everywhere along this coast, larger and with flatter heads than common seals, ungainly and almost pitiable on the rocks but masterful in the sea.

A short route home may now be taken up the valley ahead. Here, the traces of old potato lazy beds may be discerned beneath the rough pasture. For the undaunted, beyond the small stream where yellow flag irises bloom in June, a pathway worn through the bracken steeply ascends the slope ahead

The white beacon with Sherkin beyond

This is a wild place, the sea a constant presence, the only human sign a few rocks on rocks. On these headlands, before the Famine, there were cabins of stone and turf, now ruined and almost undetectable. Dog violets grow under the bracken. There is sorrel, sharp to the taste, small breaks of primroses and a few bracken-engulfed wild daffodils in spring. In summer, sea pinks flourish on the rocks below and patches of bird's foot trefoil are draped like yellow rags on the cliff tops. At the top of the path, we reach a sort of platform where we may pause to enjoy the view before continuing to the highest point,

Hill 100, as I'll call it, requires crossing the scalp and plugging onward, a little higher. When we walk here on winter's evenings, snipe rise from underfoot, spinning and zig-zagging aloft, screeching in alarm. Paths are footworn by walkers or animals; they meander everywhere and the rambler must judge his or her way by picking the clearest routes to points ahead.

Also, these are not public paths, in the legal sense; this land is owned by farmers. Over the years, they have not obstructed walkers, but trespassers - for such we are - should be aware that the land owners owe us no 'duty of care' and we walk at our own risk. Loose dogs are out of the question; sheep graze the small fields, and can be panicked over the cliffs, or abort lambs in terror.

That said, Hill 100 is worth every step of the walk to reach it. We are, here, on top of the near world, between the sea and the sky. To the north, the hump of Mount Kid rises out of the landscape. Panning the eye west, we cross Sherkin and, beyond it, Hare Island, to Mount Gabriel, behind Schull. Mount Gabriel, site of the earliest copper mines in Western Europe, haunt of the last wolves, is still a potent presence in the landscape, the huge, white, communication "golf balls" on the summit clearly visible through binoculars; at night, it is crowned with lights. To the south west, Slievemore on Sherkin, and Cill Leice and the spine of Cape Clear

Shag, common on rocks below the Beacon

rise against the sky, seemingly all one island. The Fastnet Rock can just about be seen from some angles on the western slope.

At one time, all the sea before us was the domain of the O'Driscolls. In the 15th century, they demanded that "Every ship that fisheth....between the Fastnet Rock and the Stags (off Toe Head) is to pay ten shillings and two pence, a barrel of salt, a hogshead of wine and a dish of fish three times a day." We may stand, or sit on a rock; looking out on this vista, we will surely marvel.

(5) When filled to the brim with view and sea air, we turn northeast and pick our way downhill, on what paths we can find, through the prickly dwarf gorse and bell heather. As the map indicates, there is a road head only 400 yards, or 15 minutes, away. Walking towards it, we reach a low, overgrown stone wall and walk to the right along it. We cross it just before the "valley" between the knolls; there is a pond of run-off water here in winter.

The track, barely discernible, runs twenty feet or so outside the wall which forms the inland boundary of a series of small sheep pastures, islands of green on the headland slope. Our route heads almost straight for the signal tower a mile to the east. Now, as the path becomes more distinct and easily walkable, a large, stone-grey, slate-blue ruin is on a hillside above us to the right. We soon see the top of a blue-grey barn, and the gable of a bungalow. We arrive out in a farmyard of well-kept corrugated barns, and turn left for Baltimore, down a country lane.

Orange red montbretia blooms on the roadside ditches in August, and we have views to the left of the Ilen mouth. A spur to the left is ignored, and we pass the large, stone faced, pink gabled Rolf's Holiday Hostel and Cafe Art set in pleasant gardens. The downhill road passes between bungalows with Cordyline Australis 'cabbage' palms in front and reaches the main road. Here, we turn right and, two hundred yards along, at the green water pump and the signs for the Lifeboat Station, turn left.

This route takes us past the Aquaventure Dive centre and the Baltimore Harbour Resort to heaps of spoil, and broken shale, and massive, decaying corrugated sheds, and broken roofed warehouses. No doubt, these will shortly be replaced by new development as is the trend throughout 'millennium' Ireland.

As we walk left along the water, we pass picturesque scrapped cars, then Glenans Centre, then colourful fishermen's nets and buoys. On the pier ahead, large vessels stand dry-docked. Rounding the corner, we pass a row of tasteful, stone faced holiday cottages. Beyond them, the ruin of Fineen's Fort of the Jewels rises out of the knoll of bedrock, its crumbling stone walls and gables dwarfing the narrow street and humble houses which now separates it from the sea.

The length and breadth of Sherkin Island

Fifteen minutes by ferry but very different from the island of Ireland. History and unspoiled nature abounds.

Locality: OS Sheet 88, starting at 029258, 15 minutes by ferry from Baltimore Pier.

Description and Distance: Only one 'loop' is possible on Sherkin, the circle taking in Horseshoe and Kinish harbours. Otherwise, we walk to northern, southern and western extremes, and retrace our steps. Total distance, 9 miles, readily divided into shorter sections.

Walking Time: 4 hours. Early afternoon crossings, returning to the mainland on the last boat, allows time for longer or shorter sections, even for the entire walk.

Walking conditions: Some green paths and the rest almost all narrow, metalled roads with cars rarely seen.

Features: The peace and slow pace of an offshore island. An ancient abbey and castle, in ruins. Pleasant bathing beaches and all but traffic-less roads.

Flora and fauna: Notable seashore flora. Some rare flowers.

Equipment: Comfortable shoes.

Itinerary:

(1) Sherkin is only 15 minutes from the mainland but the very air has a different 'feel'. We step off the boat into a world reminiscent of the 1950s. The absence of cars doesn't alone explain this. There is something 'island' about Sherkin. Perhaps it is that feeling of isolation from the world which, until the recent past, prevailed throughout the entire island of Ireland   In this

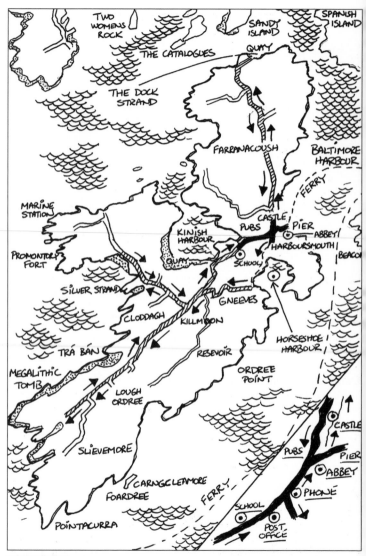

Sherkin Walk

sense, a visit to Sherkin takes one back in time. Inside the houses, there are power showers, TVs, phones and computers but the lanes and the landscape seem suffused with a slower time.

A steep road leads up from the pier, past a ruined abbey. Overnight visitors set off carrying their luggage; there are no taxis to meet them. New sounds surround us, bird-song and bee-hum, sounds that pervade the island air everywhere in summer. Swallows twitter on the wires. Butterflies seem tamer and more numerous.

Arriving on an early afternoon boat, we have more than enough time to walk the length and breadth of Sherkin, and to pause at suitable intervals to drink it in. If we arrive in the morning, we will also have time, weather permitting, for a swim, and a sundowner at the pub before leaving the island. Let there be no hurry; just to stand on the pier and watch the small pollock thread through the weed and the crabs hang on the pier wall as they fish is enough to while away time most pleasantly. When the children are young, and the tide is in, it is likely they will immensely enjoy diving into the deep, clear waters and will never want to go home.

Above the pier, the abbey, a Franciscan house founded by the O'Driscolls in about 1460, is roofless but well restored by the Office of Public Works. In 1537, it was burnt by Waterford raiders, smarting from the expropriation of two and a half thousand gallons of wine by Fineen O'Driscoll from a Waterford-bound ship that sheltered in the harbour earlier that year. The Waterford English force 'invaded', took the castle, and spent five days ravaging the island, burning the villages, abbey and castle, and scuttling or seizing the O'Driscoll fleet. Sir Fineen, as he later became for a while, lived on long enough to lend support to the Spanish/Irish cause at Kinsale in 1601, to lose his lands for his trouble and to die destitute in his castle at Lough Hyne.

The plants on the earth and stone wall on our left as we walk towards the telephone box and the shop are worth notice. Here, amongst others, may be found Sherkin's only crop of Bird's Foot, a rare, small white flower of

Dead Nettle, in flower

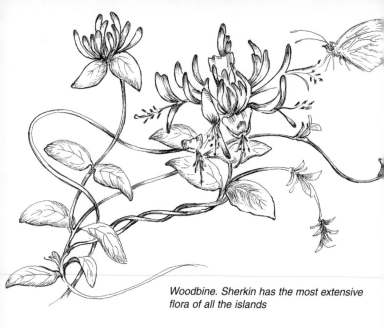

Woodbine. Sherkin has the most extensive flora of all the islands

early March. Sherkin has the largest flora of all the islands of the bay, the most trees and the best developed scrubland.

(2) For afternoon walkers who like the western sun in the face, the sensible option is to take the road to the north first and then go south west. To do this, we turn right after the abbey and set off up the road passing between The Jolly Roger and the big, new pub and accommodation units on the right. Just beyond, a right turn takes us down to the castle.

At the O'Driscoll castle, now a few ivy covered walls and a stumpy tower looking across at Baltimore, some ancient culinary plants may be found, once staples of the castle kitchen garden. Wild black mustard (with yellow flowers), wild parsley (on the walls), and tall, celery-like Alexanders flourish, and an old apple tree. One can imagine Sir Fineen, the rover and pirate, sending for a leaf of mustard to go with his poached salmon in 1537. That March, as the first flowers of the mustard showed, life should have been looking up for Fineen. Wine galore to go with his salmon and the O'Driscoll's still able to levy a fee for any boat, from any port, fishing between the Stags and the Fastnet Rock.

Back on the tarmac, the road winds gently north, between high ditches, with views across the water to Ringarogy and Spanish Island and its few small fields of sheep. On black rocks, shabby-looking cormorants congregate, hanging out their black wings to dry. All spring and summer, the background sounds are bird song and the humming of bees. Sherkin is 'the peaceful kingdom', unique in this modern age. New houses are being built, above marshy ground brilliant with flag iris in May. The houses are on the sites of ruins, and have legitimacy; it isn't new houses so much as cars that we visitors and walkers need fear. Busy roads would destroy Sherkin as we know it. But the island's future is for the islanders to decide.

We top a small rise and see rocks and islands laid out before us, Sandy, The Catalogues, Heir, and Turk Head. From late March, these are ablaze with gorse; beyond them, channels of bright water, blue hills and the bulk of Mount Gabriel where, nearly 4000 years ago, the Irish mined copper before any other Europeans and, mixing it with tin imported from Cornwall, made bronze. Now, huge, white 'golf balls', monitoring North Atlantic air and sea traffic, top the summit.

The roadway leads down to a short boat slip, called The Dock, and a small beach with a wide expanse of sand exposed at low tide, enabling one to walk to what would, otherwise, be offshore islets. The small cove is a delight for the amateur naturalist or the child with a shrimping net. The pocket Sherkin Island Marine Station Publication, "A Beginner's Guide to Ireland's Seashore" is invaluable. Sherkin has its own imprint, under the aegis of Matt Murphy, a dedicated Irish environmentalist who came to live on the island, raised a large family and founded an extensive and highly respected research station. His quarterly Sherkin Comment newspaper covers marine topics from around the globe, while the Marine Station publication "The Wild Plants of Sherkin, Cape Clear and adjacent islands" is a major contribution to the literature of Irish flora.

Low water in the cove provides a chance to see most of the common seaweeds of Ireland's shores. Each algae has its own niche

Kinish

and occupies a specific zone, nearer or further from the tide mark. High and dry, ten feet up the rock walls on the left, channelled wrack survives in the high water splash zone; moisture held in the channels on the fronds keeps it alive for days. At the base of the rocks, sugar kelp, like flattened barley sugar, and oarweed, a kelp with a strong stipe or stem, is submerged at all but the lowest tides. Elsewhere in this small cove, almost the entire inshore flora may be found, the various wracks, sea lettuce, laver, edible carageen and so on.

The rock pools contain liver-red anemones with brilliant blue 'beads' around the 'neck' from which the tentacles emerge; they tickle your fingers 'electrically' if you touch them. In summer, there are small fish, shannies and gobies, also, crabs and prawns. Shellfish abound - thousands of tiny, white acorn barnacles on the rocks, limpets, like cones, between them, periwinkles, with black, snail-like shells, and dogwhelks, similar, but cream coloured, with a groove at the shell opening allowing a small 'snorkel' to be raised as they crawl over mud. When I find whelks adhered to mussel shells, I am always tempted to remove them; with a drill-like tongue, they bore into the soft body of the unfortunate bivalve which, of course, cannot escape. Note the number and variety of shells we find on the beach with a neat hole drilled in them!

These sands are also the homes of exotic marine worms. Sand masons put up tubes of sand, fringed with a sandy mop to protect the delicate tentacles they raise to trap food when the tide covers them. The spaghetti-like whorls of lugworms are everywhere, with a hole close by; the worm is a foot beneath the sand, roughly between the two.

(3) We return to the Abbey corner the way we came. Unfortunately, there is no 'loop' but, coming from a different angle, we may see things that were hidden as we first passed.

(4) At the corner, we turn right, towards the telephone box and the general store; there is framed map of the island on the right. At the phone box, we turn left, taking the sign for Horseshoe Harbour. This is an unpaved lane. We pass a ruin to left, possibly once part of the abbey, now a stone gable with a gaping window, and Horseshoe Cottage, a B&B imaginatively festooned with nets and net-balls. After a gate, the lane goes right, between the cottage and the sea. We can see why the mirror-calm amphitheatre of water below us is named for a horseshoe, its mouth opening to the sea. We cross a stile and the path is good, a green road. Tall foxgloves hang over it in June, and bees buzz busily in the sun trap of the laneway. The heather and gorse covered slopes and the deep blue of the harbour make this circuit a summer idyll. A few pretty houses edge the lane or look down on it, houses reachable only on foot. Blackthorn blooms over the water in March, whitethorn in May, montbretia in August, fuschia into October - never a colourless day once spring has come.

The path descends. At the lowest point, there are terraces of soft grass over the sea, fine for lying on or laying out a picnic of a summer day. In winter storms, they are a good vantage point from which to watch the wild waves breaking over the harbour mouth. A stream crosses the path, muddy in wet weather, before it climbs the slope to Gneeves on the south side.

As we climb, we can see, across the harbour, the small Sherkin lighthouse and its attendant cottage. Reaching the top, we come upon a shale road into a house and turn right along it, views opening up of houses on the headlands and of the church, with its bell arch, beside the tarmac road in the middle distance with the Atlantic and the islands out beyond. This is the road we will take, straight, shining in the sun and running south west.

We pass a pond, a rarity on Sherkin, with spike rush, flag iris and scrub willow; if mink haven't reached Sherkin, one would expect to find waterhens (called 'moorhens' in Britain) nesting here. Kinish Harbour, with, again, a narrow mouth, is now seen. We pass a break of trees on the left - sally and scrub willow - and some pines on the right. Trees are rare on the islands. A pair of opportunistic magpies annually build their domed nest of twigs in the middle.

We reach the water, a sheltered lagoon cut off by a low wall, covered at high tide, from Kinish. Here, in the muffled silence of a misty March afternoon, we watched four pairs of mergansers courting on the flat calm water two hundred yards from the road Mergansers are amongst our loveliest ducks, rakish in appearance, with a crown like a wild crew-cut. Largely sea faring, they are not often seen close inshore. In courtship ritual, the black-headed males bob like clockwork toys, swell their breasts and throw their beaks skywards. The red headed female modestly cruise between them.
Trees arch over the road ahead and we pass through a dappled, leafy tunnel.

One Sunday, children from a house alongside came to sell us 'magic stones' and to show us their tadpoles. We pass new council houses, pastel-bright on the landscape and grey, venerable ruins that fade into it. We ignore the road to the right, and continue south-west, direction Trá Bán, walking into the afternoon sun. The house beside the church has a remarkable tree, like a macracarpa, the crown wind flattened. Then, the priest's house and the church, with its three arched windows and bell arch above the gable. On the roadside walls, crispy lungwort lichen flourishes on the stones, with sea ivory, a grey lichen with stiff, flat branches up to two inches long and nodules - the reproductive bodies - at the tips. This lichen is tolerant of salt spray. Mount Gabriel looms large on the distant north west skyline; nearer true north, in the middle distance, a castle stands lonely on the mainland shore. Cape Clear Island comes into view ahead, with its signal tower. Now, below us on the right, a good sand beach, horseshoe-shaped Trá Bán, the "white strand". The road is straight and trafficless. The islands to the north are Heir Islands, the three Calfs, and beyond, Castle Island and Long Island, beside Schull.

Sherkin is Inis Archáin, Archain's Island. Who or what Archain was is unknown; we may say the meaning is "arcane". It was possibly St Kieran of nearby Clear Island or possibly 'orcas', whales or porpoises, sometimes seen.

The road divides in a Y; we follow the grassy track, the right 'arm', past an old stone house and down towards the sea. Black rocks lie between us an Clear Island, which rises very high, with the signal tower and houses sil-

The Abbey, burnt by Waterford raiders in 1537

All that remains of Fineen The Rover O' Driscoll's castle

houetted against the sky. With binoculars, we can see the road climbing the hill, and follow the progress of the rare car on the island.

(5) We must, of course, go back the way we have come. However, the views are different - in the middle distance, we have the sweep of West Bay to the north, with its two sandy beaches, enclosed by Drowlaun Point. Beyond the second beach, Silver Strand, long, low buildings are part of the Marine Station, housing a veritable university of the sea in huts and annexes reached by tracks across unshorn fields. Here are libraries of books and data, and high tech labs where biologists study fish, fowls and flowers. At one time, the public could visit and view a sea aquarium but the high cost of insurance, resulting from Ireland's 'compo' culture, has forced it to close.

(6) After passing the church, we take the road to the left, signposted Silver Strand. We shortly arrive at an 'isthmus', with Kinish Harbour on our right and the beaches on our left. At low tide, hardly a square foot of the muddy 'strand' of Kinish is without a worm cast. As in the case of The Lag at Ringarogy, a metre of healthy Irish slob contains more invertebrate life that a cubic metre of Amazon rain forest; it's easy to believe it here too, at Docknaganee.

The road is often white with blown sand and a path leads onto Silver Strand,

A Grey Heron
("Johnny -" or "Judy - the -bogs")

a very pleasant and popular bathing beach in summer. In the evening, the western light glances off the roofs of Cape Clear across the Gascanane Sound. Continuing north, we pass a road to the left, leading to the Marine Station and an ancient promontory fort. The road straight ahead takes us to close views of Heir Island, Inishodriscol. As there is no 'loop' route, we must retrace our steps.

(7) Our route back to the boat takes us, again, past Kinish. Herons and Ireland's new birds, little egrets, fish the shallows. There is a spinney of holly and Scots pine in a field on our right. We see the neat school-house ahead. "Sherkin Male National School, 1892", says a plaque in front wall and at the rear, another plaque announces, "Sherkin Island Girls' and Boys' National School 1892 - 1992". Sacred Heart and Virgin Mary statutes can be seen through the windows.

Can there be a lovelier spot for teaching or for learning? With the calm waters of Kinish on three sides, amidst the "blossom'd furze, unprofitably gay", island masters and mistresses have taught generations of pupils at this little school. At the time of writing, six or eight children still attend.

There are houses on Kinish with large yachts drawn up beside the gardens; the harbour must be deep at high tides. We pass the Community Centre, and the library. A feature of this stretch in summer is puffing-and-panting holi-day makers with their children and luggage rushing for the boat. Visitors tend to wait until the last minute. It is hard to leave Silver Strand, the island and its peace.

Below, on the left, Rugher Strand fills with fat, slow mullet at full tide. We top the rise, and head downhill towards the abbey and the pier. If we are early for the boat, we may divert to the pubs for post-amble drinks. Hospitable and relaxed, they afford views of Baltimore and the approaching boat. At the pier, the children beg for "a last swim", don trunks and leap into the deep, clear water. Sometimes, in summer, the bay is full of mackerel as we cross, with white terns screaming and, further out, big, white, cruciform gannets, with black wing tips, diving on the shoals.